Table of Contents

Be A Thermostat Anger Management Workbook

Nola C. Veazie, Ph.D., CADC-II

To order additional copies, please contact us.
V-Solutions Consulting, LLC
www.vsolutionsconsulting.com

Session1: Overview of Anger Management

In this session you will explore the concept of anger as a secondary emotion and discuss general assumptions. This includes internal and external attributions, cognitive appraisals, and environmental cues. This session covers the following:

I.   Purpose of the group/class

    1) Learn to manage anger effectively

    2) Identify environmental cues

    3) Explore assumptions

    4) Develop self-control over thoughts

    5) Distinction between anger and aggression

    6) Gauging the intensity of your anger

    7) Warm up exercise

II.   Group/class rules

    1) Safety

    2) Confidentiality

    3) Assignments

    4) Absences and cancellations

III.   Definition of the terms

What is Anger?

The American Psychological Association characterized anger as "antagonism toward someone you believe have done you wrong." Deater-Deckard and Wang (2013) added that anger can be conceptualized from a "state-emotion" perspective. In other words, people's anger is simply a result of their state of mind or emotional viewpoint. Current anger management research describes this construct as a cognitive process that affects how people perceive the world. In plain language, anger is based on a representation of our view of the world. Nature and nurture affect the way we think and thus influences our reaction to environmental stimuli. For example, some people are easily angered while others respond calmly to the same situation. The difference in response may largely relate to the person's appraisal of the situation.

The literature on anger management suggests that people's interpretation of their environment is primarily a result of information and experience garnered. Adding to this knowledge, Josephs and McLeod (2014) proposed that individuals with anger management problems believe their assessment of their own and the other person's mental state is correct. For example, "I have a right to be angry with Sue for missing my daughter's party. This point of view is reinforced by my appraisal of Sue's state of mind. For instance, I believe that Sue purposefully forgot to attend the party because she deemed it unimportant. According to the authors, our interpretation of the mental state of others reflects attributions or misattributions that expose our own assumptions. What does this all mean? Attributions are inferences we make about what caused an event or behavior. When Sue missed the birthday party, I attributed her behavior to a lack of caring. Thus, Sue's behavior is seen through the lens of internal attributions; her behavior is related to her feelings toward me.

Remember, the choices we make are often based on assumptions (Veazie, 2006). Please take some time to reflect on the following questions: What assumptions about people trigger uncontrolled anger? What assumptions about anger contribute to negative appraisals? Jot down your thoughts here:

_____

_____

_____

_____

_____

_____

_____

_____

_____

_____

_____

_____

_____

Attributions

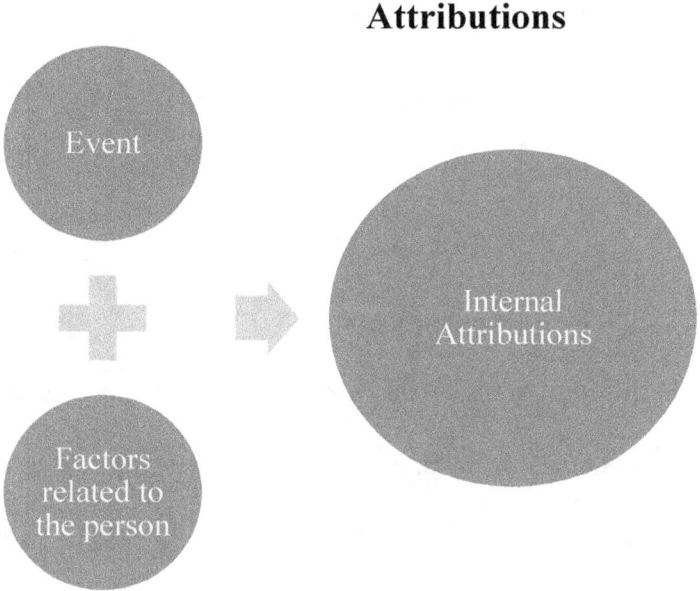

Figure 1: **Internal Attribution**
*Based on inferences about a person's traits, abilities, attitudes, or even stereotypes.

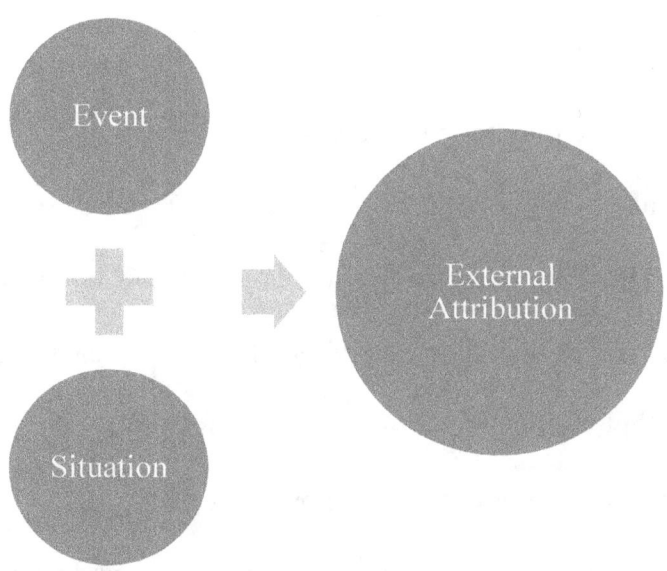

Figure 2: **External Attribution**.
*Based on the situation or environment

Getting Started

The goal of anger management is manifold. Understanding the distinction between anger and aggression is paramount. Some people believe anger leads to aggression and violence; thus, they tend to bury their anger. . According to Josephs and McLeod (2014), anger management reduces emotional feelings and the physiological arousal that causes anger to escalate, thereby producing negative behaviors. Additionally, anger management programs engage participants in an exploration of cognitive distortions, assumptions, and misattributions that cloud judgment and may lead to violence. The Substance Abuse and Mental Health Service Administration defined anger as "a feeling or emotion that ranges from mild irritation to intense fury and rage." Conversely, aggression leads to injury and property damage. How you define anger is important because it determines how you deal with it. Remember the movie anger management with Adam Sandler? Dave Buznik (Sandler's character) was wrongly sentenced to anger management classes. The stewardess and a fellow traveler on the plane repeatedly told Dave that he had a problem with anger, when he was merely asserting himself with another passenger. He became increasingly agitated when everyone around him (including the judge) insisted that his anger was out of control. The movie concluded with a very important lesson; Dave Buznik learned that persistent bullying by others and inability to speak up caused an undercurrent of resentment that ignited repressed anger. Moreover, Dave's failure to address the bullying caused him to repress his anger, which later manifested physically, emotionally, and behaviorally.

Unlike Dave Buznik, you may not have trouble expressing your anger. Perhaps you immediately respond to bullying or manipulation; however, your anger may get out of control, or you bury it. This workbook will improve your understanding of the physical, emotional, and spiritual effects of anger. Moreover, it outlines the consequences of uncontrolled anger. Each exercise will challenge irrational thinking and negative cognitive appraisals that incite anger, increase the likelihood of poor communication, and cause strained relationships. You will also learn techniques that foment physical, emotional, and spiritual wellbeing. Start each class or group by checking in and sharing your daily strategies for dealing with anger. Use the table on the following page to determine the activating event (situation) believed to have triggered your response and identify internal or external cues. An external cue could be someone yelling, a person you dislike, a song, a smell, or even your surroundings. On the other hand, internal cues refer to thought processes. What are your thoughts about the situation? What is your current emotional state? Remember, your response to a given situation may be subjective and linked to how you feel at that moment. Internal and external cues often affect our appraisals of events.

Cues are indicators or signs that trigger thoughts, emotions, or behaviors. When we hear an old song it triggers good or bad memories and takes us back to a different place or time in history. Smells elicit the same response; certain spices, pine trees, or fruit cake, bring back memories of Christmas. Unfortunately, some cues elicit memories of abuse or violence and causes some people to become defensive or retreat. Pay close attention to your internal and external cues and discuss strategies to facilitate positive outcomes.

Warm-up Exercise

The following exercise aims to engage participants in a discussion about anger through story-telling. After completing the exercise use post-it notes to record your expectations for the class. How will you know when you have accomplished your goals? Identify specific issues you want to work on.

Step I: The instructor will pair participants in dyads and select a speaker and a listener. Have the speaker describe a challenge or situation in which he/she became so angry it resulted in an argument, fight, or negative consequence. If the participant is not comfortable discussing their own story, they can give an example of another situation. Participants may say something like "dealing with _____ is a challenge for me because...." I became so angry, I ......"

Step II: Bring each pair into a larger group of 4, 6, or 8 people. Have the listener from each dyad summarize the story told by the speaker. Each group should choose 1-3 stories and discuss the activating event, belief system, and consequences. Point out irrational or self-defeating thinking that sustained negative behaviors, ambivalence, and unresolved anger.

Step III: Select a speaker from each group of 4-6 participants to summarize one of the stories; include the context, challenges, feelings, and consequences. The group representative should also discuss why the group chose their particular story. Members from other groups have an opportunity to weigh in on the discussion. The instructor can tailor the exercise to suit the needs of the group.

Table 1

Anger check-in © By V-Solutions Consulting		
ACTIVATING EVENT	INTERNAL AND EXTERNAL SIGNALS	ANGER MANAGEMENT STRATEGIES

*Use the above table to assist participants to check-in during each session

Defining Anger

How do you define your Anger?

_____

_____

_____

_____

_____

_____

How did your family of origin define anger?

_____

_____

_____

_____

_____

_____

_____

_____

What internal cues (signals) trigger an angry response?

_____

_____

_____

_____

_____

_____

_____

What external cues trigger angry response?

_____

_____

_____

_____

_____

_____

_____

How does your definition of anger affect how you deal with it?

_____

_____

_____

_____

_____

_____

_____

Use the anger meter to gauge your anger; discuss your score

_____

_____

_____

_____

_____

_____

_____

List external attributions

_____

_____

_____

_____

_____

_____

List internal attributions

_____

_____

_____

_____

_____

_____

_____

_____

Anger Meter

- Outburst

- Violence

- Loss of control

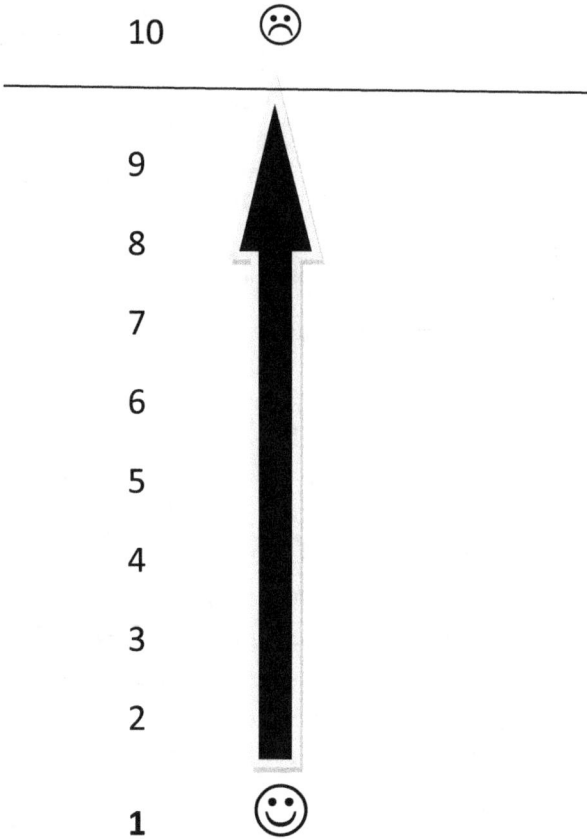

- Make better choices
- Use your anger control plan to avoid reaching 10!
- Use problem solving skills

Figure 1: **Anger Indicator**

Notes

Session 2: Effects of anger

Uncontrolled anger has a physiological, psychological, and spiritual effect on the individual and negatively influences relationships. This negative expression of anger curtails effective communication. On the other hand, repressed anger smolders and slowly erodes our ability to effectively express feelings. In this session you will learn about:

I.   The ABC's of anger

        1) Activating event

        2) Belief system

        3) Consequences

II.   Address the physiological, psychological, and spiritual effects of anger

III.   Understand repressed anger

IV.   Identify cognitive appraisals

Anger has a physiological and psychological effect on people! Moreover, uncontrolled anger results in cognitive distortions, irrational thinking, and negative appraisals. For example, allowing anger to spiral out of control affect how you evaluate and interpret events and may lead to damaging consequences. A cursory review of the situation will likely suggest that someone or something, other than yourself, caused you to behave badly. In fact, your belief about the event may be the culprit, prompting a negative response. Your behavior may be excessive even though the situation is relatively benign. Let's look at the following example:

1. **Activating event:** The situation or what happened. "My partner did not acknowledge that I cleaned the house."

2. **Belief system:** Your thoughts about the event. "He/she does not value me or the things I do."

3. **Consequence:** What happened as a result of your reaction or response? "I blew up and called him/her demeaning names"

Research in the field of cognitive behavioral interventions proposed that cognition (thinking) control external behavior. This workbook uses Cognitive Behavioral Interventions (CBI) to address dysfunctional thinking, maladaptive behaviors, and cognitive processes that move anger from a relatively normal response to rage, and potentially escalate to violence. Each exercise will increase your comfort level and help you address how you feel and deal with anger. More importantly, these exercises are designed to tap into unconscious feelings, cultural beliefs, and attitudes that reinforce how you address emotions.

Use the ABCs of anger exercise, on the following page, to jot down your belief about an event and your reaction to the event. After completing the exercise, use this page to describe the event, explore your belief system, and consequences in greater detail. What happened as a result of your reaction?

_____

_____

_____

_____

_____

_____

_____

_____

_____

_____

_____

_____

_____

_____

_____

_____

_____

_____

Table 2: ABC's of Anger

Activating Event	Belief System	Consequence

*This table employs the biblical principle (as a man thinks so is he) and Albert Ellis' Rational Emotive Behavior concepts.

Repressed Anger

Some people are unaware of their anger because they unconsciously bury it. Repressed anger is like an impending volcanic explosion ready to unleash smoldering lava that will harm those in close proximity. This form of anger lay dormant beneath the surface for months or even years before erupting at inopportune times. Most people are surprised when they lose control; citing that the intensity of their anger caught them off guard. Can you think of a time in which the intensity of your anger did not match the severity of the situation? What were your thoughts? Were you aware that you were angry?

Addressing repressed anger is difficult; your anger is buried for good reason. Anger covers feelings of guilt or shame that threaten to expose vulnerabilities. Thus, you may feel that exposing these feelings will cause psychological harm; opting instead to leave them buried. Sometimes masked feelings of guilt and shame are funneled through cognitive appraisals and manifests as uncontrolled anger (see fig 4). Consequently, primary emotions such as guilt and shame give way to more powerful emotions. Anger (the more powerful emotion) serves a short term purpose but increases the complexity of reconciling how you view yourself in contrast to the intense emotional reaction others see.

What are cognitive appraisals? Lazarus and Folkman (1984) proposed that cognitive appraisals are mental processes that create stress. Repressed anger negatively affects cognition and therefore how we appraise events. Moreover, stress further degrades our ability to manage anger and thus creates a cycle of negativity.

Primary and Secondary Emotions

Create a list of primary and secondary emotions.

Primary Emotions   **Secondary Emotions**

_____   _____

_____   _____

_____   _____

_____   _____

_____   _____

_____   _____

Describe each primary and secondary emotion; which category affected you most?

_____

_____

_____

_____

_____

_____

_____

_____

Cognitive Appraisals

Powerful emotions, such as anger, affect how we evaluate the world and thus contribute to how we interact with people. The following exercise provides an opportunity to assess each scenario and identify cognitive appraisals. Read the following case carefully and see if you can pick out the thinking that may have contributed to the fight.

Martha and John are college sweethearts who recently got into a big fight because John cancelled a dinner date. When Martha approached John about the cancellation, he minimized her concerns. Martha's best friend recently broke up with her boyfriend and was bad mouthing men in general. Joyce (Martha's friend) seized every opportunity to remind Martha that men are "no good" and will hurt her. Although John never gave Martha a reason to doubt him, his response during the fight, coupled with Joyce's negative talk made Martha nervous. Martha told John that she wants to call off their engagement and have nothing to do with him. What are some of the negative appraisals that fueled the fight? Did Martha overreact? Did Martha's angry reaction have merit?

_____

_____

_____

_____

_____

_____

_____

_____

Figure 2: **Primary Emotions Funneled Through Cognitive Appraisals**

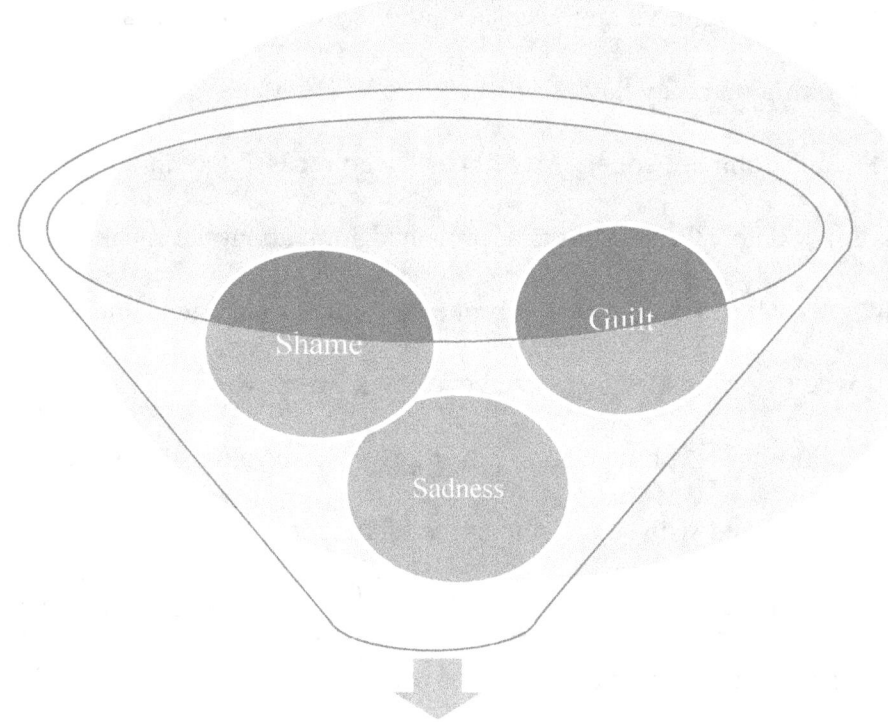

Uncontrolled Anger

What is repressed anger?

_____
_____
_____
_____
_____
_____
_____

What is below the surface of your anger?

_____
_____
_____
_____
_____
_____
_____
_____

I get angry when

_____
_____
_____
_____
_____
_____
_____

What is the common denominator when you lose control?

_____
_____
_____
_____
_____
_____
_____

Notes

Session 3: Cost and payoff of anger

According to Novaco (1994) anger has a polarizing duality that makes it difficult to reconcile. This construct can be disruptive yet energizing or destructive yet empowering. This duality makes it difficult for people to embrace anger and deal with it in an appropriate way. Anger provides a payoff in the form of power; however, your new found power may cost your physical, emotional, spiritual, and relational wellbeing. In this session you will learn about:

I.   Cost and payoff of anger

    1) Repressed anger

    2) Uncontrolled anger

    3) Duality of anger

II.   Anger management exercise

    1) Cost and payoff

    2) Rose exercise

    3) Two minute anger drill

Cost and Payoff of Repressed and Uncontrolled Anger

There is a cost and payoff of embracing repressed and uncontrolled anger. The literature is replete with information dealing with the consequences of repressed anger. For example, an article written by Elena Conis (2003) revealed that researchers proposed a link between repressed anger and headaches. In practical terms, people who repress their anger are more likely to have chronic headaches. Although this and other articles cite the cost of dealing with repressed anger, the dearth of information regarding the payoff of anger limits our understanding of the subject.

The literature clearly cites the cost of repressed and uncontrolled anger, but does anger offer a payoff? Yes, uncontrolled and repressed anger offer a payoff. What happens when you get angry? You yell, slam the door, and make yourself bigger than the other person. Consequently, the other person becomes intimidated and may back down. Thus, the payoff for uncontrolled anger is keeping someone at bay. What is the payoff of repressing your anger? The fear of addressing hurt or pain with a person who may react violently may lead you to repress anger. Trepidation about being perceived in a negative light may also lead to repress emotions. People are often exposed to situations or activating events, which leaves them feeling good or bad about the encounter. When we view events through the lens of repressed anger, we appraise them more negatively.

Cost and Payoff of Repressed Anger

Figure 3: Negative appraisals that sustain repressed anger

Addressing the Cost and Payoff of Anger

Cost:_____

_____

_____

_____

_____

_____

_____

_____

_____

_____

_____

_____

_____

_____

_____

Payoff:_____

_____

_____

_____

_____

_____

_____

_____

_____

_____

_____

_____

_____

_____

_____

_____

*Use the rose exercise on the next page to explore what your anger say about you

The Rose Metaphor

© by Eugenia Campbell

Roses are beautiful! What part of the rose are you most like?

_____

_____

_____

_____

_____

How is your anger like the thorns on a rose?

_____

_____

_____

_____

_____

How do the thorns on your rose help?

_____

_____

_____

_____

_____

How do they hurt or hinder relationships?

_____

_____

_____

_____

Are the thorns the cost or payoff?

_____

_____

_____

_____

The Two Minute Anger Drill

The two minute anger drill is based on Nancy and Donald Tubesing's (1983) structured exercises in their stress management book. In this exercise, participants pair up to answer a series of questions regarding how they currently deal with anger or have dealt with anger in the past. The instructor asks participants to pair up with someone who's last or first name begin with the same first letter. You can use a variation; for example, pair participants by birth month. Participants will:

1) Find a partner

2) Designate one partner as cost and the other as payoff (or another description that fits the lesson)

3) Participants face each other and take turns asking the following questions, or come up with your own questions.

    A. What is the greatest payoff of uncontrolled or repressed anger?

    B. Was it a short or long term benefit?

    C. What is the greatest cost of expressing anger in an uncontrolled fashion?

    D. What would you change?

4) After two minutes switch roles. For example, Cost asks the questions in the first two minutes and payoff asks the questions in the last two minutes. Remember you can ask the same questions as many times in the two minutes (determine if the answers change).

5) After each participant has an opportunity to answer questions, the instructor will bring the group together. Discuss what participants learned about the cost and payoff of dealing with uncontrolled anger.

Notes

Session 4: Labeling Emotions

We use labels in all facets of life to describe or refer to things, people, and situations. We also use labels to describe emotions. Some people have a hard time identifying and labeling their emotions. Vine and Aldao (2014) believes this impoverish emotional labeling is associated with a deficit in regulating emotions. In this session, you will learn to label primary and secondary emotions. The session will center on the following:

I.   Appropriately labeling our feelings

    1) Using emotional emoticons to discuss feelings

    2) Sentence completion exercise

    3) Primary and secondary emotions

II.   Reframing

    1) Using reframing to diffuse heightened emotions

    2) Positively framing anger

    3) Dissonance

Labeling our Feelings

Labeling the way we feel is not an easy task. Emotions don't always match facial expressions, body language, or even behavior. The mismatch between what we feel and people's reactions to our feelings create dissonance or conflict. For example, Lisa felt sad because her husband (Donald) said something that hurt her feelings. Consequently, she became upset and referred to Donald by a derogatory term, prior to slamming the door. In turn, Donald left the house without apologizing. Lisa's reaction did not garner the response she expected. Her reaction masked her sadness, leaving Donald to incorrectly assess the core meaning of her behavior.

In the previous example, Lisa's inability to express her sadness led to an angry outburst. Unfortunately, her reaction prompted Donald to have a negative appraisal of the situation and shut down communication. Primary emotions reveal our vulnerabilities; therefore, they are often buried and seldom recognized. On the contrary, secondary emotions are more powerful and thus more visible. For example, the expression of sadness may be construed as weakness. Appearing weak or vulnerable may not be seen as a viable option, even when the alternative keeps us from achieving our goal.

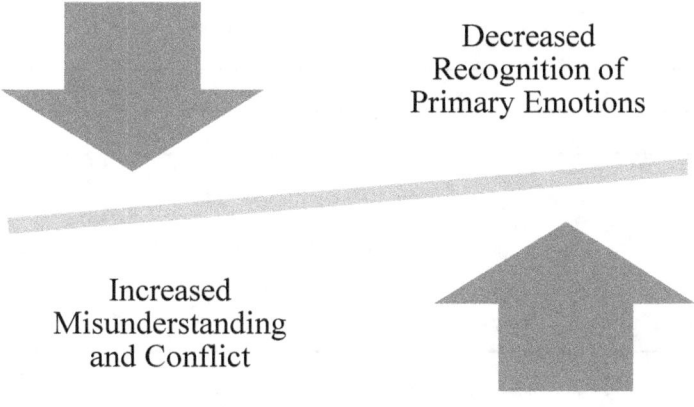

Decreased
Recognition of
Primary Emotions

Increased
Misunderstanding
and Conflict

As stated earlier, pinpointing primary emotions is difficult. Correctly labeling feelings require skill and the courage to confront them. Now that you are more comfortable talking about feelings, use the following exercise to appropriately label them. Write a short description of how you feel next to the emoticon that best describes your mood.

Figure 4: Emotion Emoticons

_____

_____

_____

_____

_____

_____

_____

_____

_____

_____

_____

_____

_____

_____

_____

_____

_____

_____

_____

_____

_____

_____

_____

_____

_____

_____

_____

_____

_____

_____

The following exercise will help you identify your feeling and address them in the proper context. Some feelings are outside of our awareness and may manifest as anger, frustration, or disappointment. However, what you may be feeling is sadness, loneliness, or worry. Secondary emotions mask deeper more vulnerable feelings and may lead to conflict when not properly addressed.

What are you feeling at the moment?

_____

_____

_____

_____

How is your anger different from feelings of fear?

_____

_____

_____

_____

How do people in your family of origin deal with sadness?

_____

_____

_____

_____

How do people in your family of origin deal with anger?

_____

_____

_____

_____

Do you deal differently with the above emotions?

_____

_____

_____

_____

Reframing

A picture is worth a thousand words! We live in a self-absorbed world in which people spend an inordinate amount of time taking self-portraits called selfies. From this vantage point, we've become self-absorbed with superficial concerns such as finding our best angle, but avoid dealing with deeper emotional issues. Selfies often remain in a permanent state of suspension in our cell phones, not unlike repressed anger and some primary emotions.

This next exercise gives you an opportunity to reframe your anger by placing it into appropriately labeled frames. You place your emotional selfies in the proper context or frame when you address primary emotions. Frames beautify, give a unique look to pictures, and disguise a bad picture. On the other hand, a psychological frame provide context to our emotions. Clinicians describe frames or frame of references as schemas or beliefs/values used to infer meaning. Changing the frame or frame of reference changes inferred meaning. In the previous example Lisa initially labeled Donald's behavior as lack of caring, which led to sadness, disappointment, and ultimately uncontrolled anger. How might Lisa react if she reframed her thinking? What if Lisa believed that Donald was joking or being insensitive, rather than trying to hurt her? Would her response be different?

Take a selfie, create an emoji, or use emoticons in figure 4 to reflect daily or weekly emotion. Reframe your feelings by cutting and pasting each selfie or emoticon in the frame that represents your new frame of reference. Identify the reasons you chose each selfie or emoticon. Answer the following questions prior to completing the reframing exercise.

How do I feel right now?

_____
_____
_____
_____
_____
_____
_____
_____
_____
_____
_____
_____

What assumptions guide my thinking?

_____
_____
_____
_____
_____
_____
_____
_____
_____
_____
_____
_____

How do I create change?

_____
_____
_____
_____
_____
_____
_____
_____
_____
_____
_____
_____

Reframing Exercise

Happy

Sad

Angry

Confused

43

Worried

Content

(Insert Emotion)

(Insert Emotion)

The exercise on the previous pages gave you an opportunity to reframe beliefs that perpetuated uncontrolled and repressed anger. You were encouraged to view your feelings through alternative lens and thereby reframe them. For example, you can reframe a problem as an opportunity to grow, unkindness as a lack of understanding, and a weakness as strength in training.

The following sentence completion exercise taps your unconscious to reveal attitudes about anger.

A. When _____ happens I feel _____

B. When someone treats me wrong I feel _____

C. When I see _____, I feel _____

D. Being angry means _____

E. Being sad means _____

F. Being happy means _____

G. When I think about_____, I feel _____

H. People who_____

I. Make me feel_____

1. Explain your reaction to what you saw in your reframing collage

_____
_____
_____
_____
_____
_____
_____
_____
_____
_____
_____
_____
_____
_____

2. Identify who or what triggered each emotional episode (positive or negative).

_____
_____
_____
_____
_____
_____
_____
_____
_____
_____
_____
_____
_____
_____
_____
_____

3. Write a poem expressing your emotional state of mind.

_____
_____
_____

_____
_____
_____
_____
_____
_____
_____
_____
_____
_____
_____
_____

4. Introspection helps evaluate internal emotions. Reflect on your inner feelings and thoughts and describe them here.

_____
_____
_____
_____
_____
_____
_____
_____
_____
_____

5. What did you learn about yourself that you did not know prior to this exercise?

_____
_____
_____
_____
_____
_____
_____
_____
_____
_____

Notes

Session 5: Anger and Conflict

Conflict is inevitable because of divergent points of view. Webster's dictionary defined conflict as being antagonistic, incompatible, a fight or war, disagreement, or emotional disturbance. Regardless of how we define conflict, it has an integrative (brings people together) or distributive (divides) effect. During this session, you will discuss the following:

I.   Types of conflict

II.   Dynamics

III.   Conflict styles

   1) Avoiding

   2) Smoothing

   3) Bargaining

   4) Forcing

   5) Problem solving

IV.   Effective communication

Anger and Conflict

Some dictionaries define conflict as antagonism, incompatibility, disagreement, or emotional disturbance. Regardless of the definition, the literature outlines two dynamics (integrative and distributive) that can influence the outcome. Anger-laden conflict seldom brings resolution to a problem. This form of conflict is distributive in nature and it is based on a win-lose notion. The philosophy behind this form of conflict is, the more one party gets, the less the other can have. Inevitably, a distributive dynamic produces a winner and loser, and creates a cycle of escalating conflict. Conversely, an integrative approach establishes a positive cycle of cooperation among individuals.

The notion that conflict is always bad discounts the power of effective communication and conflict resolution. Viewing conflict as all bad reflects the idea that everyone should think and feel the same. Although we are equal in the eyes of the law, we are unique in the eyes of God. The word unique emphasizes divergent views, but also speaks to our ability to create synergy and innovation. What do I mean? People are different and therefore, process information differently. Conflict arises when an individual is unable to effectively convey his/her difference of opinion to another person. We allow conflict to further escalate if we ignore primary emotions or use ineffective conflict resolution styles.

Conflict styles are as varied as our personalities; according to the literature on conflict resolution, these styles bring resolution or further escalate conflict. However, five conflict styles are predominant in the literature (collaborating, compromising, accommodating, competing, and avoiding). For the purpose of this workbook, I will use nomenclature found in Dr. Marshall Sashkin's conflict style inventory to describe these styles. Dr. Sashkin proposed that people use avoiding, smoothing (accommodating), bargaining, forcing (competing), and problem solving (collaborating) to address conflict. We do not exclusively use one style over another; however, people lean more toward one style during periods of heightened stress.

Results from Dr. Sashkin's conflict inventory revealed that using avoiding as a conflict resolution style tells the other person that you are withdrawing from the conflict. The bottom line is one person has capitulated to his/her opponent. Using this style of conflict resolution may mean leaving the outcome to chance or to simply give up. Avoiding conflict, however, has its merits; this style maybe appropriate when:

1. Your preferred outcome is not realistically possible. For example, external barriers such as distance, time, or policies will likely prevent a resolution.

2. What you lose by avoiding the conflict is much less than what you might lose by using any of the other strategies. Others may see this as a "trade-off"

3. Emotions are running too high. Remember Lisa and Donald? It may have been better for Lisa or Donald to call a time out rather than allow their emotions to escalate.

4. More information could lead to better quality solution: Postponing a decision or discussion until all relevant information has been obtained is useful.

Describe a situation in which you used **avoiding** in addressing conflict:

_____

_____

_____

_____

_____

_____

The second conflict resolution style is smoothing. Use of this style promotes covering up and pretending that everything is ok. People use smoothing if the other person's anger is out of control and you fear it may escalate to violence. Partners in volatile or violent relationship sometimes use smoothing to calm the other person down. When all parties to a conflict openly participate in smoothing, it is labeled **agreeing to disagree**. Smoothing is not a long-term strategy because the underlying problem goes unresolved. This problem resolution style can be beneficial when:

1. Open conflict might have a negative effect on the current situation or escalate to violence. **If you are in a violent relationship, the best option is to safely exit.**

2. When a positive outcome is unlikely. If you are not really concerned about the issue, but the other person is, you might smooth over the situation to maintain a positive relationship with the other person. If you don't have a pony in the race, why argue about the outcome?

3. If you're going to lose anyway and rather cut your losses.

4. Violence is not ok and smoothing rarely stops violence

Describe a situation in which you used **smoothing** to address conflict:

_____

_____

_____

_____

_____

_____

The third conflict resolution style is forcing. According to Dr. Marshall Sashkin, if smoothing is a passive form of conflict resolution, forcing is the most aggressive style. This style engages both parties in a full-fledged battle for control and creates a lose-lose situation. People who use forcing as their primary style to resolve conflict engage in stereotyping others and discount their uniqueness. For example, "I must force my values on a particular group, otherwise they won't get it." This style is seldom productive and creates a stressful environment. However, like other styles forcing can be helpful. For example, this style is useful when:

1. This strategy is most useful when you must take immediate action because the situation is extremely important (making a decision involves life or limb)

2. When the other side is determined and aggressive and the issue cannot be tabled

3. If the issue involves a basic principle that cannot be compromised or abandoned

Describe a situation in which you used **forcing** to address conflict

_____

_____

_____

_____

_____

_____

_____

The fourth conflict resolution style is bargaining. This involves negotiation for the purpose of reaching a trade-off. Each party agrees to compromise in an attempt to gain advantage. Bargaining may involve a mediator or arbitrator and it is useful when:

1. Each party gives and gets something.

2. When it's not worth the effort of the conflict, the issue is not all that important.

3. When there's no common goal. If the parties to a conflict refuse to back down and have aims that are impossible to reconcile; it may still be possible to find a compromise that gives each something they want

4. When the parties feel pressure to reach some agreement

Describe a situation in which you used **bargaining** to address conflict:

_____

_____

_____

_____

_____

_____

_____

_____

_____

_____

The fifth and final conflict resolution style is considered the most effective. Problem solving consists of using a number of methods in an orderly fashion to find a solution to problems. Unfortunately, angry people are not very good problem solvers; in fact, anger is associated with interpersonal conflict. This strategy, also considered confronting, is used by individuals who recognize that a problem exist and agree to collaborate to resolve it. Problem solving is useful when:

1) All involved recognize that the problem can only be resolved by using creative solutions that satisfies all parties

2) When it is important to gain a consensus and commitment to resolve a common problem

3) When your objective is to test your assumptions and learn or understand the views of others. This technique contributes to building empathy

4) To merge insights from people with different perspectives on a problem

5) To work through hard feelings that have been interfering with an interpersonal relationship

Describe a situation in which you used **problem solving** to address conflict:

_____

_____

_____

_____

_____

_____

Dealing with Conflict

How do you define conflict?

_____

_____

_____

_____

_____

_____

_____

How do you manage conflict?

_____

_____

_____

_____

_____

_____

_____

_____

Conflict Style Exercise

Describe a situation in which you used the following conflict styles, and explain the outcome of the situation.

Avoiding

_____

_____

_____

_____

_____

What was the outcome?

_____

_____

_____

_____

_____

Bargaining

_____

_____

_____

_____

What was the outcome?

_____

_____

_____

_____

Smoothing (accommodating)

_____

_____

_____

_____

What was the outcome?

_____

_____

_____

_____

Forcing (competing)

_____

_____

_____

_____

_____

What was the outcome?

_____

_____

_____

_____

_____

Problem Solving

_____

_____

_____

_____

_____

What was the outcome?

_____

_____

_____

_____

_____

Conflict Style Observer Sheet

This is an excellent exercise to do in small groups. Have each group select two people to role play. Participants will replay a situation that created conflict. Individuals engaged in the role play may select a topic of discussion or the instructor/facilitator can provide one of the case studies outlined in this book. You will select one member to be an observer. The observer will jot down information, elements, and interactions that match each of the five styles outlined below.

Avoiding/Withdrawing

_____

_____

_____

_____

_____

_____

Smoothing

_____

_____

_____

_____

_____

_____

Forcing

_____

_____

_____

_____

_____

Bargaining

_____

_____

_____

_____

_____

Problem Solving

_____

_____

_____

_____

Notes

Session 6: Thermostat versus Thermometer

Thermometers are instruments designed to measure or indicate temperature. The mercury in a thermometer rises or falls as it adjusts to external or internal conditions. Conversely, a thermostat regulates the temperature by adjusting it from hot to cold or vice versa (Veazie, 2006). During this session you will look at your anger through the lens of a thermometer or thermostat and learn how each perspective affects how you deal with anger.

I.   Definition

II.   Difference between a thermostat and a thermometer

III.   Irrational thinking

IV.   Changing thinking errors

V.   Change talk

VI.   Exercises (Anger management commercial)

Describe the difference between a thermometer and a thermostat

_____
_____
_____
_____
_____
_____
_____
_____

Describe an activating event

_____
_____
_____
_____
_____
_____
_____
_____

How would you describe the event from the standpoint of a thermometer?

_____
_____
_____
_____
_____
_____
_____
_____

How would you describe the event from the standpoint of a thermostat?

_____
_____
_____
_____
_____
_____
_____
_____

Use the sample thermometer and thermostat on the next page to describe an event. For example, talk about an event that did not turn out the way you expected. Were you a thermostat or a thermometer? Describe specific behaviors: "I got into an argument and I said or did_____"

_____

_____

_____

_____

_____

_____

_____

_____

_____

_____

_____

_____

_____

_____

_____

Thermometer versus Thermostat

The thermometer: The situation determines your behavior. You read the emotional temperature and react. Describe the goal of your anger. Do you have control? Why or why not?

The thermostat: You regulate the outcome of your circumstances. If the prevailing emotional temperature is hot, you cool things down by responding rather than reacting. How do you control your anger by acting as a thermostat?

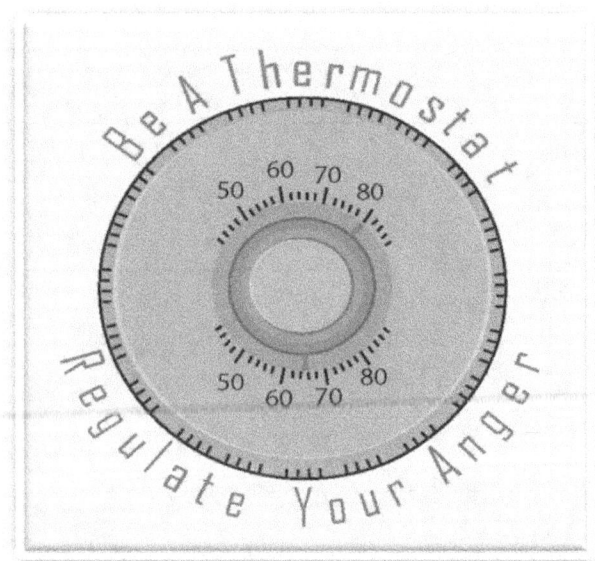

Irrational Thinking

A number of theories propose that certain thinking frameworks lead to anger and negative behavior. However, identifying, labeling, and dissecting irrational thoughts empowers the individual to change negative outcomes. Anger management uses cognitive behavioral techniques that increase awareness about how thinking affects behavior and consequently determines decision-making. Our thoughts elicit feelings and subsequently cause us to behave in certain ways (we think, we feel, & we behave). What if you could change unwanted behavior by changing your thoughts? What if you expressed anger appropriately by simply monitoring your thinking? What are some irrational frameworks that may lead to uncontrolled expression of anger?

I. Catastrophizing: Seeing things in the worst possible light and forecasting most awful outcome. For example, a fight with your spouse or a friend may be seen as the end of the relationship rather than a bump in the road.

II. Minimizing: The other side of the coin. When we catastrophize, we blow things out of proportion. Conversely, when we minimize we dismiss the other person's feelings or point of view. Minimizing devalues the other person. For example, sharing your feelings with someone who dismisses you or responds by saying "yes but" discounts your point of view.

III. Personalization: This is a form of grandiosity, which places you at the center of the reason for another person's behavior. For example, someone walked pass you without acknowledging you may lead to the belief that he/she is angry with you.

IV. Jumping to conclusion: Making logic-based statements before gathering all the facts may lead you to believe that you know what another person is thinking. How many times have you jumped to conclusions about another person's behavior only to find out you were wrong? For example, "my best friend did not call me today, she must be angry." What if he/she was sick or busy? How have the following irrational thought patterns influence your level of anger in the past? Unfortunately, jumping to conclusion maybe the only exercise some people will engage in.

Research suggests that behavior is learned and can therefore be unlearned. Thus, techniques that solely focus on behavioral change use external contingencies such as shaping, contractual contingencies, or time out to produce change. What about the thinking that sustains such behavior? Irrational thinking fuels anger and often leads to negative outcomes. This type of thinking results in harmful consequences, but does not have to. This workbook uses cognitive behavioral techniques to challenge cognitive appraisals, thinking errors, and assumptions that reinforce uncontrolled anger.

The following sentence completion exercise offers an opportunity to describe thinking deemed irrational. Talk about irrational thinking and how it influence behavior. Give specific examples and describe the outcome of such thinking (how it influenced your behavior). Describe the thinking, the subsequent feeling, and the behavior.

Catastrophizing

_____

_____

_____

_____

_____

Minimizing

_____

_____

_____

_____

_____

Personalization

_____

_____

_____

_____

_____

Jumping to conclusion

_____

_____

_____

_____

_____

Changing Thinking Errors

Think ▶ Feel ▶ Behave

What am I thinking?

_____

_____

_____

_____

How does it make me feel?

_____

_____

_____

_____

How does my thinking influence my behavior?

_____

_____

_____

_____

Producing Change Talk

Change talk is any conversation that communicates the desire or readiness to move toward change. Changing irrational thinking is difficult but not impossible. Motivational Interviewing uses a number of cognitive techniques to produce and sustain change talk (Rollnick, 1983). One technique uses the acronym DARN-C (desire, ability, reasons, need and commitment). For example, you can use the acronym as follows:

➤ Use open-ended questions to ascertain desire to change, ability to change, reason to change, need to change, and commitment to change

➤ Ask the person to elaborate

➤ Ask how were things better or different as a result of the change

➤ Ask what may happen if things continue the way they are

➤ What is the worst thing that might happen if you don't change

➤ On a scale from zero to ten, how important is it to make a change? Follow up by asking why the person chose five instead of zero.

➤ Ask about the person's guiding values. For example, what are your life goals? Follow up by asking, how does your behavior fit outlined goals? "So Lisa, you said you want Donald to share his feelings with you, but you fly off the handle anytime he does." Is it more important to be right? Or, is it more important to be more intimate?

Change Talk Exercise

Desirability for change

_____

_____

_____

_____

Ability to change

_____

_____

_____

_____

Reason for change

_____

_____

_____

_____

Needing to change

_____

_____

_____

_____

ABC's of Cognitive Behavior

Activating event_____

Belief (thinking)_____

Consequence (behavior)_____

You can't always change the activating event but you can change your belief or feelings and thus affect the outcome or behavior

Negative Thinking

Increase Positive
Behavior

Give 3 ways in which you can decrease negative thinking and increase positive behaviors

1.

2.

3.

Give 3 examples of negative thinking that affected your behavior/outcome

1.

2.

3.

Give 3 examples of positive thinking that affected your behavior/outcome

1.

2.

3.

ANGER MANAGEMENT COMMERCIAL

Out-of-control anger has become more prevalent. Road rage and other anger fueled behaviors lead to violence.   Today I would like you to create a new anger management product that will assist people with either channeling their anger appropriately or moving from being a thermometer to a thermostat. You can be as created as you like. After inventing the product, create a 2-3 minute commercial about the product and make a sales pitch to the audience.

References

Conis, A. T. (2003, Jul 27). REPRESSED ANGER COULD BE FUELING THAT HEADACHE. *South Florida Sun - Sentinel* Retrieved from http://search.proquest.com/docview/387803918?accountid=458

Josephs, L., & McLeod, B. A. (2014). A theory of mind–focused approach to anger management. *Psychoanalytic Psychology, 31*(1), 68-83. doi:http://dx.doi.org/10.1037/a0034175

McDermott, R. C., Schwartz, J. P., & Trevathan-Minnis, M. (2012). Predicting men's anger management: Relationships with gender role journey and entitlement. *Psychology of Men & Masculinity, 13*(1), 49-64. doi:http://dx.doi.org/10.1037/a0022689

Novaco, Raymond W. (1994). Anger as a risk factor for violence among the mentally disordered. In J. Monahan and H. J. Stedman's (Eds), *Violence and mental disorders: Developments in risk assessment.* Chicago: The University of Chicago Press.

Tubesing, N., & Tubesing, D. (1983). Structured exercise in stress management. Duluth, Minnesota: Whole Person Press.